Author Luigi Pruneti
Translator Paul Clark

Series Editor Giovanni Caselli
Book Editor Penny Clarke

Created, designed and producced by
Studio Illibill, Florence, Italy

Illustrations by
Claudia Saraceni, Thomas Trojer

Published by
PETER BEDRICK BOOKS
156 Fifth Avenue
New York, NY 10010

Published by agreement with
Macdonald Young Books Ltd, England

Library of Congress Cataloging-in-
Publication Data

Pruneti, Luigi.
    Viking explorers / Luigi Pruneti. –
1st American ed.
        p. cm.– (Voyages of discovery)
    Includes index.
    Summary: An illustrated survey of
the early history of the Vikings, focusing
on sea exploration, ships, navigation
methods, and trade routes.
    ISBN 0-87226-486-6
    1. Vikings–Juvenile literature.
2. Northmen–Juvenile literature.
[1. Vikings.]   I. Title.   II. Series.
DL65.P78 1996
948′.022–dc20   96–33
                                  CIP
                                   AC

Second printing, 1998

Printed in Hong Kong

VIKING
Explorers

PETER BEDRICK BOOKS
NEW YORK

CONTENTS

Words that are explained in the
Glossary are printed in **bold** type the
first time they are used on a spread.

INTRODUCTION

The Vikings, the people of Scandinavia, dominated the seas of northern Europe for some 300 years. They were known all over Europe as fierce barbarian warriors and ruthless pirates. Nowhere was safe from them. They were such skilled sailors that, even without compasses, they could make long ocean voyages. They could sail far inland up rivers because their boats were so shallow.

But the Vikings had not always been like this. Until the end of the 8th century they had lived quite peacefully in the part of northern Europe we call Scandinavia. There they fished and farmed the rather poor land. No-one knows why they suddenly became the scourge of Europe. Perhaps their population had grown so much that fishing and farming could no longer feed everyone. The fact that the Vikings stole farm animals and grain, as well as gold and silver treasures, suggests this could be a reason.

Do the Vikings deserve their reputation? Some may have been fierce and ruthless raiders, but others were superb craftsmen. The raiding voyages would have been impossible without well-built, water-tight boats. Metalworkers may have made deadly weapons, but they also made beautiful jewelry. And when the Vikings settled in other lands, such as Russia and France, they mixed so well with the local people that they soon became part of the community. All this rather contradicts the popular view of Vikings as barbaric, ruthless pirates. So why do we think of them like this? Probably because all the surviving accounts of the Vikings' raids are written from the point of view of the victims. Clearly, a fleet of longships sailing upriver, or about to land near a lonely monastery, was a terrifying sight. Many monks wrote vivid accounts of these raids. But, because few Vikings could read or write, there are no accounts of just how exciting the raids were, or how difficult and dangerous. And it is only quite recently that archaeologists have confirmed that the Vikings did reach North America, something primitive barbarians could not have done!

Europe before the Vikings

In the 8th century (AD 700-800) a large, powerful state grew up in western Europe. It covered an area that is now made up of Germany, France and much of northern Italy. Its ruler was Charlemagne (742-814).

Although this state was very big, its population was small. The largest towns were little more than villages. The excellent roads built by the Romans some 600 year earlier had disappeared or were in such a bad state they were difficult to use. This made communications between the various parts of Charlemagne's lands slow.

Charlemagne, however, was a very strong ruler. He defeated the **Muslims** from North Africa who had conquered Spain and were attacking Europe. He also stopped the fighting between the different European peoples and saved Pope Leo III from being overthrown by his enemies.

Under Charlemagne it seemed as if Europe was to have peace for the first time since the collapse of the Roman Empire nearly four centuries earlier. But the peace did not last. When Charlemagne died in 814, a new threat faced Europe: the Vikings.

THE BRITISH ISLES were divided into many small kingdoms, which were frequently at war with each other.

North Sea

BRITISH ISLES

THE VIKINGS destroyed Charlemagne's capital late in the 9th century. The modern German city of Aachen is on its site.

Aachen

CHARLEMAGNE commanded a large army. The **cavalry** was well equipped and heavily armed.

THE CITY OF TOLEDO in Spain was famous for its weapons.

Pyrenees

SPAIN

Toledo

Cordoba

Seville

Granada

Mediterranean Sea

AFTER CONQUERING most of Spain, the Muslims crossed the Pyrenees and threatened the south-western borders of Charlemagne's lands in France.

NORTH AFRICA

THE MUSLIMS had come from North Africa. They were fierce and skillful warriors and were not driven out of Spain until the 15th century.

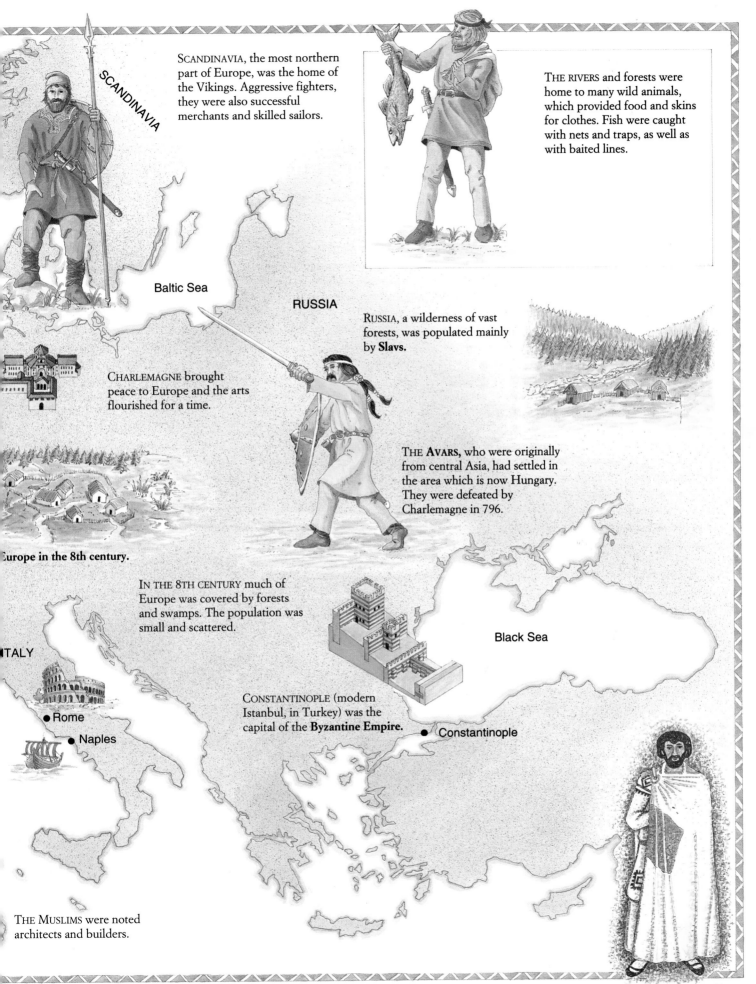

SCANDINAVIA, the most northern part of Europe, was the home of the Vikings. Aggressive fighters, they were also successful merchants and skilled sailors.

THE RIVERS and forests were home to many wild animals, which provided food and skins for clothes. Fish were caught with nets and traps, as well as with baited lines.

Baltic Sea

RUSSIA

RUSSIA, a wilderness of vast forests, was populated mainly by **Slavs.**

CHARLEMAGNE brought peace to Europe and the arts flourished for a time.

THE **AVARS,** who were originally from central Asia, had settled in the area which is now Hungary. They were defeated by Charlemagne in 796.

Europe in the 8th century.

IN THE 8TH CENTURY much of Europe was covered by forests and swamps. The population was small and scattered.

Black Sea

ITALY

● Rome

● Naples

CONSTANTINOPLE (modern Istanbul, in Turkey) was the capital of the **Byzantine Empire.**

● Constantinople

THE MUSLIMS were noted architects and builders.

7

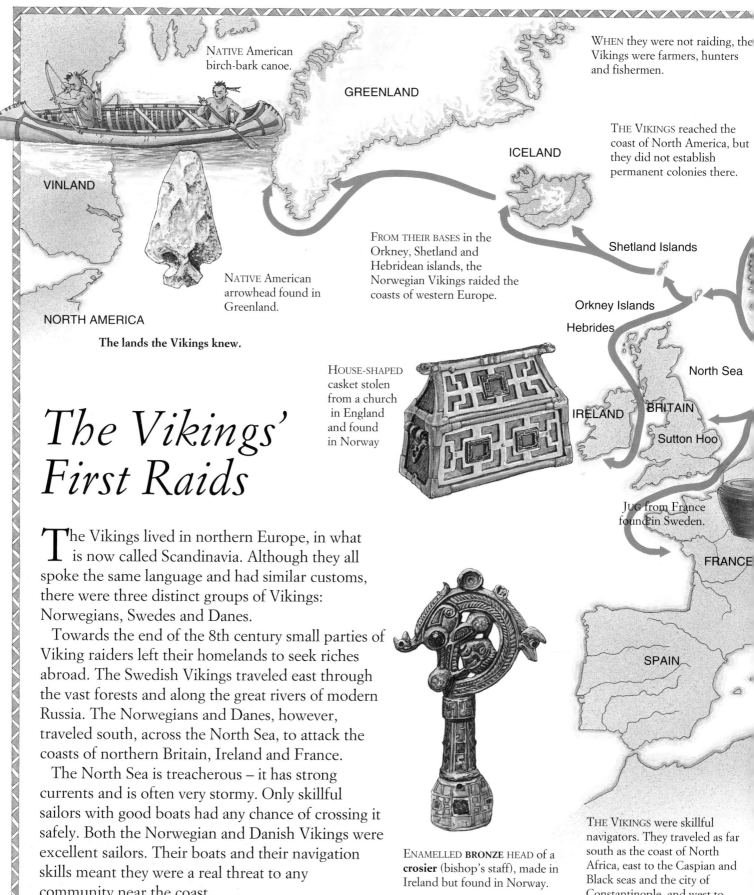

NATIVE American birch-bark canoe.

GREENLAND

WHEN they were not raiding, the Vikings were farmers, hunters and fishermen.

ICELAND

THE VIKINGS reached the coast of North America, but they did not establish permanent colonies there.

Shetland Islands

VINLAND

NATIVE American arrowhead found in Greenland.

FROM THEIR BASES in the Orkney, Shetland and Hebridean islands, the Norwegian Vikings raided the coasts of western Europe.

Orkney Islands

NORTH AMERICA

Hebrides

The lands the Vikings knew.

North Sea

HOUSE-SHAPED casket stolen from a church in England and found in Norway

IRELAND   BRITAIN

The Vikings' First Raids

Sutton Hoo

JUG from France found in Sweden.

FRANCE

The Vikings lived in northern Europe, in what is now called Scandinavia. Although they all spoke the same language and had similar customs, there were three distinct groups of Vikings: Norwegians, Swedes and Danes.

Towards the end of the 8th century small parties of Viking raiders left their homelands to seek riches abroad. The Swedish Vikings traveled east through the vast forests and along the great rivers of modern Russia. The Norwegians and Danes, however, traveled south, across the North Sea, to attack the coasts of northern Britain, Ireland and France.

The North Sea is treacherous – it has strong currents and is often very stormy. Only skillful sailors with good boats had any chance of crossing it safely. Both the Norwegian and Danish Vikings were excellent sailors. Their boats and their navigation skills meant they were a real threat to any community near the coast.

SPAIN

ENAMELLED **BRONZE** HEAD of a **crosier** (bishop's staff), made in Ireland but found in Norway.

THE VIKINGS were skillful navigators. They traveled as far south as the coast of North Africa, east to the Caspian and Black seas and the city of Constantinople, and west to Iceland, Greenland and the North American coast.

THE SWEDISH VIKINGS were successful merchants, establishing trade centers and settlements in Russia.

SWEDEN

SCANDINAVIA

THE DANISH VIKINGS preferred to raid the rich lands of France and Britain.

Baltic Sea

MANY

ITALY

SCANDINAVIAN SILVER PENDANT discovered in Russia.

SMALL STATUE OF BUDDHA made in central Asia but found in Scandinavia.

RUSSIA

Caspian Sea

Konugard (Kiev)

Black Sea

GERMAN GLASS VESSELS found in Sweden.

Constantinople

Mediterranean Sea

Baghdad

ARABIA

NORTH AFRICA

BRONZE **BRAZIER** made in Baghdad (Iraq) and found in Sweden.

ARABIAN SILVER COINS found in Norway.

A SCENE from the Bayeux tapestry shows the Normans building a boat in preparation for the attack on England.

THE **PROWS** OF VIKING LONGSHIPS were decorated with a carving of a monstrous figure. The Vikings believed that the monster would frighten away the gods protecting the places they were about to attack. When they were sailing near friendly coasts, the figure was removed, so it did not upset the local gods.

VIKING BOATBUILDERS chose the trees for their boats with great care. They had to be tall and straight.

Viking Ships

The Vikings used different types of boat for different purposes. For journeys of exploration and raiding across seas and up rivers they used the longship or **drakkar**. These boats were long and narrow, about 100 feet in length and barely 16 feet wide. They were also very shallow. These characteristics helped the boats ride big ocean waves, as well as making them ideal for sailing inland up rivers.

PINE, FIR AND OAK were the woods most commonly used by the Vikings for their boats.

THE VIKINGS' LONGSHIPS were built by highly skilled, specialized craftsmen. There were **caulkers, carpenters** and smiths and they used a wide variety of tools, among them: **augers,** axes, saws, files, knives, planes, gouges, scrapers, hammers, chisels and pliers.

THE SHIPS' MASTS had to be very strong to withstand storms at sea. They were usually between 60 and 65 feet in length.

THE JOIN between a branch and the trunk was used to strengthen the boat.

SHIPYARDS grew up in **fjords** and deep bays, wherever there was calm water and a village or farm nearby.

A TREE WAS MISSHAPEN, the boatbuilders could still use it.

Carpenters

CARPENTERS shaping a piece of timber.

Specialized carpenter

Building a Viking longship.

Master builder

THE KEEL was the most important part of a boat and was made from a single tree trunk. This gave the boat strength and flexibility, which were important to ensure it withstood ocean storms.

A WAR STANDARD that once decorated the prow of a Viking longship. It is made of gold-plated bronze.

Navigation table

Navigation

The climate of Scandinavia is harsh, with long, cold winters and short, cool summers. Sea conditions are also bad, with severe winter storms. As a result the Vikings made their raiding voyages during the summer. Longer voyages of exploration also began in summer, but these Viking explorers spent the winter wherever they had landed before the winter storms began.

The greatest problem the Vikings faced on their long voyages was navigation. They did not have the compass which would have helped them find their position at sea when they were out of sight of land. Instead, they relied on the sun by day, knowing that it rose in the east and set in the west. At night the Vikings used their knowledge of the stars to provide the same information about their position at sea.

When it was cloudy or there was no moon, the Viking sailors had other clues to help them know where they were. The strength and direction of winds and currents were very important. Knowing the habits of sea creatures, such as seabirds, fish and whales, also helped. Some seabirds spend all year at sea, only returning to the land to breed, so, in the autumn, sailors would know the birds were flying away from land.

Iron anchor

TO FIND OUT THEIR POSITION at sea the Vikings used a navigation table. The central needle allowed them to measure the height of the sun and a movable bar pointing to the notched edge of the table showed the course they were following.

THE VIKINGS used different types of anchor to ensure they could moor their boats safely. They used rope and chain to secure the anchor to the boat.

Viking ships

Rudder

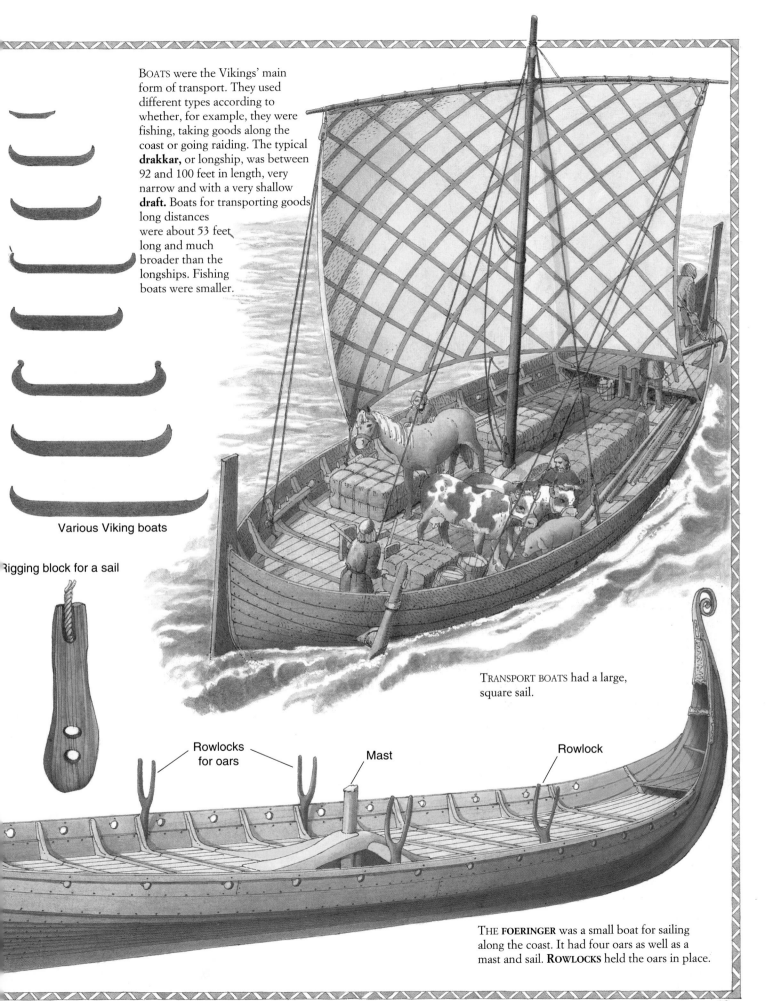

BOATS were the Vikings' main form of transport. They used different types according to whether, for example, they were fishing, taking goods along the coast or going raiding. The typical **drakkar,** or longship, was between 92 and 100 feet in length, very narrow and with a very shallow **draft.** Boats for transporting goods long distances were about 53 feet long and much broader than the longships. Fishing boats were smaller.

Various Viking boats

Rigging block for a sail

TRANSPORT BOATS had a large, square sail.

Rowlocks for oars

Mast

Rowlock

THE **FOERINGER** was a small boat for sailing along the coast. It had four oars as well as a mast and sail. **ROWLOCKS** held the oars in place.

A Viking Home

Although the Vikings were great sailors and traders, they were primarily farmers. As well as its land, each **farm** had a farmhouse, barn, forge, dairy and boat-shed. The farmhouse was the heart of every farm, where the owner and his family lived. Thick walls gave protection against the cold. There were no windows, only occasional slits covered by a semi-transparent pig's bladder. The house had a few rooms, but the large communal hall, with its central fireplace was the most important part. Benches around the walls were used as seats by day and beds by night. Sometimes cooking was done on the central hearth, but the farmhouses of wealthy farmers often had a separate kitchen with a hearth-oven.

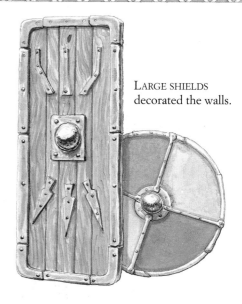

LARGE SHIELDS decorated the walls.

THE ROOF of a Viking house was covered with straw, wooden tiles and large squares of turf.

ALL VIKING MEN wore beards which they often plaited.

WOODEN SPOONS AND BOWLS were used for eating.

MEN'S CLOTHING was tough and practical. They wore long, woolen underpants, wide trousers and a tunic which reached to mid-thigh. Over the tunic went a long-sleeved shirt. To complete his dress, a Viking wore a **felt** cap, a cloak fixed by a brooch on his right shoulder, a leather belt and leather shoes.

THE VIKINGS drank from horns which were usually decorated with metal bands.

THE WALLS of the house were made of wooden planks fixed into the ground and then plastered with mud and straw. When wood was scarce, the Vikings used **peat** instead. The walls of peat were often up to 7 feet thick.

MEN, AS WELL AS WOMEN, wore jewelry: pins, necklaces, bracelets and brooches. Many pieces of Viking jewelry survive and show what fine craftsmen they were. Working in gold, silver or bronze, the craftsmen often copied jewelry imported from southern Europe.

GOLD AND SILVER arm-rings from Denmark.

A FINE BROOCH to fasten a woman's dress.

MEN fastened their cloaks with ring-pins like this, as well as with brooches.

A typical Viking house.

LARGE HEARTH-OVEN for cooking.

THE OWNER of the house sat on a raised chair in the hall.

WOMEN wore dresses that reached to their feet, with a belt around the waist. Viking families were large, so to make feeding a baby easier, dresses had two slits closed with brooches at the breasts. A large apron and thick woolen shawl to wear outdoors completed a woman's dress.

THE FIREPLACE in the middle of the central hall was very simple and had no chimney.

Viking Raiders

The Vikings were not just skillful sailors. The Norwegian and Danish Vikings, in particular, were fierce and successful raiders, too. They planned their raiding voyages very carefully. As well as food and water, they took plenty of weapons, but surprise and the speed of their raids were their two most important weapons.

The Vikings knew that there were rich religious communities near the coasts of northern Britain and Ireland. They also knew that the monks and most of the local people would be in church on Sundays, so their longships would probably not be spotted until it was too late. When they attacked, the Vikings took all the gold, silver and other treasures they could carry, before setting the place on fire. Then they returned to their ships and left almost as suddenly as they had arrived.

If the raiders discovered areas of rich farmland or good trade centres, they stayed. They built ports and settlements and used these as bases from which to launch raids on lands even further south.

EARLY VIKING ARMOR consisted of a reinforced leather shell or a **chain-mail jerkin**. Later, this was replaced by heavier, metal armor.

VIKING PORTS and settlements followed a set pattern. They were protected by **earthworks** and a **palisade.** There were two or four gates placed opposite each other and dominated by wooden look-out towers. Homes and warehouses were safe inside these defenses.

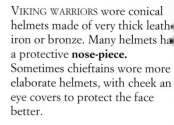

VIKING WARRIORS wore conical helmets made of very thick leather, iron or bronze. Many helmets had a protective **nose-piece.** Sometimes chieftains wore more elaborate helmets, with cheek and eye covers to protect the face better.

VIKINGS used bows made of
yew wood reinforced with
leather. According to legend,
bow strings were made from
women's hair.

THE MOST IMPORTANT Viking
gods were Baal the sun god,
Balder the good and Thor the
god of strength and thunder.
Later, Odin (right) came to be
known as the king of the gods.

CHRISTIAN
crosses made by
Viking craftsmen
showed they had
abandoned their **pagan**
beliefs.

**A fortified
Viking trading post.**

THEIR ROUND SHIELDS were
made of **lime** wood, sometimes
reinforced with metal studs.

THE VIKING WAR-AXE had
a long handle and wide blade.

THE VIKINGS' SWORDS were
lethal weapons: long and heavy,
with the blade sharpened on
both sides.

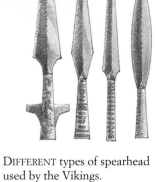

DIFFERENT types of spearhead
used by the Vikings.

The Vikings and the British Isles

The Vikings' first overseas raids were on the British Isles. In June 793 Norwegian Vikings attacked the monasteries on the island of Lindisfarne, off the Northumbrian coast, and the **monastery** of Jarrow on the mainland itself.

Two years later the Vikings returned. This time they attacked the monastery on Iona off the west coast of Scotland and monasteries on the Irish coast.

All these monasteries were important centers of Christianity and so were very wealthy. This made them ideal targets for the Vikings. Their attacks were so successful that they became an annual event. Every summer people living near the coasts watched the horizon anxiously, dreading the appearance of the Vikings' longships. Only when the autumn storms began could they relax, knowing the threat of attack was over for another year.

A GRAVESTONE showing the attack on the monastery of Lindisfarne in 793.

THE ATTACK on the monastery was so swift and unexpected that the monks had no time to defend it.

The Vikings attack Lindisfarne.

AFTER THE ATTACK the Vikings
sailed swiftly for home.

AS WELL AS gold and silver
treasures, furniture was also
taken from the monastery, along
with farm animals and grain.
Men and women who could be
sold as slaves were also valuable
prizes.

LINDISFARNE was then burned to
the ground.

ROUTES followed by
Norwegian Vikings.

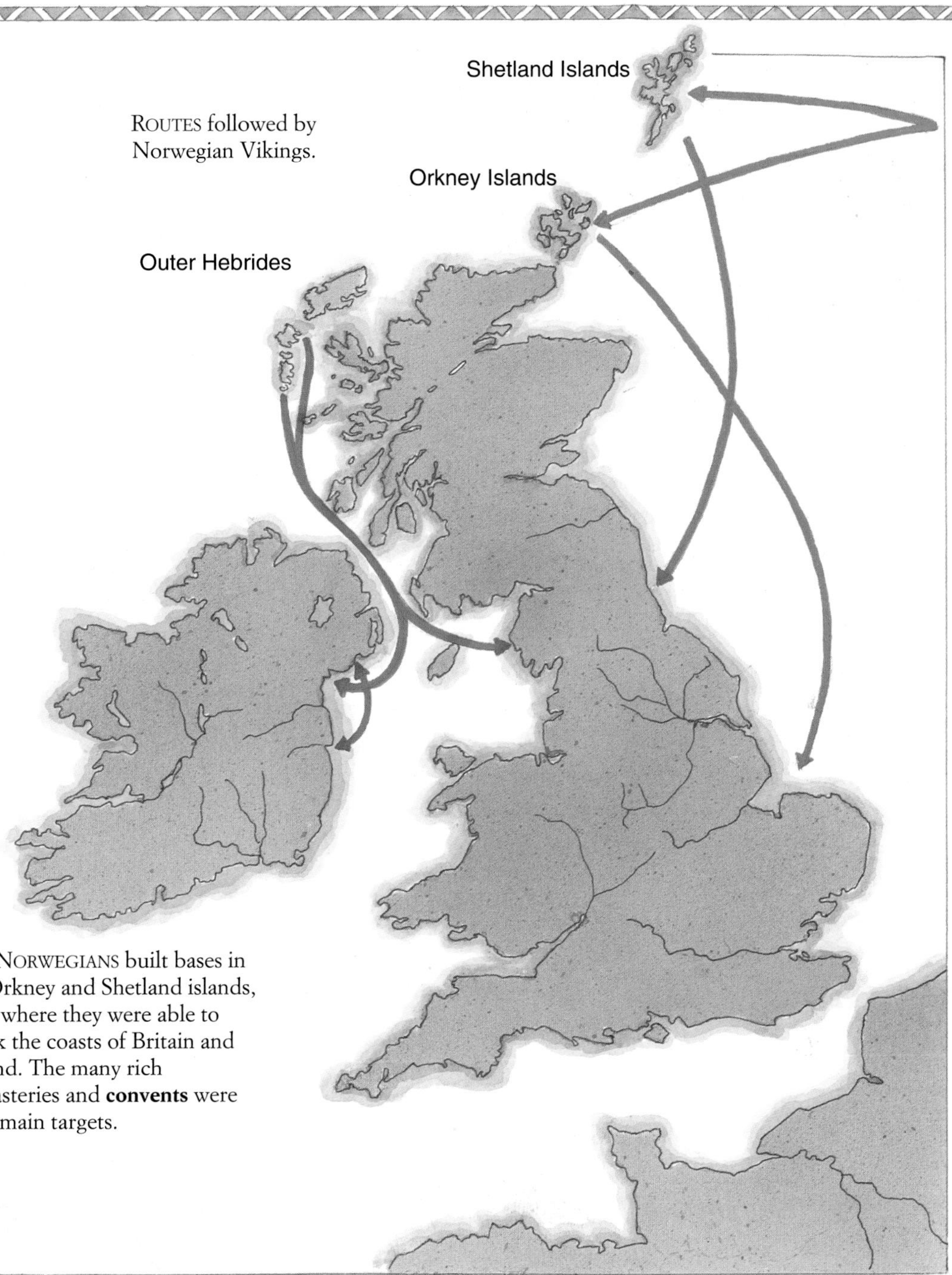

Shetland Islands

Orkney Islands

Outer Hebrides

THE NORWEGIANS built bases in
the Orkney and Shetland islands,
from where they were able to
attack the coasts of Britain and
Ireland. The many rich
monasteries and **convents** were
their main targets.

The Vikings settle in Britain

From the 8th to the 11th centuries the British Isles were the scene of many battles between the local inhabitants and the Viking attackers.

After these early encounters, the Vikings began a deliberate war of conquest. The Danes, in particular, wanted to establish settlements there. In 1013 Swein Forkbeard of Denmark and his son Cnut (sometimes called Canute) invaded England. Although they could not conquer the whole country, Cnut forced the English king, Edmund II, to divide the country, giving the Danes the eastern part, where there were already many Viking settlements. In 1027 Cnut invaded Scotland, but that campaign was not so successful.

When Edmund died in 1016 Cnut became king of the whole of England until his death in 1035. He was a strong and good ruler. He reformed the country's laws, became a Christian and encouraged trade. Under him, England was peaceful and free from more Viking attacks. As a result trade developed and it became more prosperous. Towns, too, grew up. One of these was Yorvik. Today we call it York.

A VIKING GRAVESTONE discovered in York. It is carved with an intricate design of animals.

YORVIK was well protected with earthworks, palisades and wooden towers from which the Vikings kept watch in case they were attacked.

YORVIK was an important trade centre. There were many workshops and shipyards in the town.

THE DANISH VIKINGS encouraged the building of towns in Britain. Because they were outnumbered by the local people, the Danes themselves tended to live together in towns and villages which were easy to defend.

A COIN minted in Yorvik when it was under the control of the Viking chief, Anlaf Cunune, in the 9th century.

Yorvik, the Viking city of York.

The Vikings in France

While Charlemagne was alive the Vikings did not risk attacking his lands – they were too well defended. However, when he died in 814 his heir, Louis the Pious, was too weak to defend his territories.

During earlier raids, the Danish Vikings had seen the rich farmland, prosperous towns and wide rivers of France. In 844 they attacked Toulouse, an important town on the River Garonne in central France. Before departing, they set the town alight, destroying it completely.

In the following years Nantes and Tours suffered the same fate. Although Nantes is near the sea, Tours, like Toulouse, is a long way inland. But the shallowness of the Vikings' boats made sailing up the River Loire easy.

In 885, the Danes attacked Paris, besieging it for over a year. Then, a few years later, they seized all the lands along the River Seine between the Atlantic and Paris. Their leader, Rollo, forced the French king, Charles the Simple, to sign a treaty giving these lands to the Danes.

The invaders quickly settled down to farm and converted to Christianity – just as they did in England. They integrated with the local people, becoming known as the **Normans.**

A **SEAL** depicting William the Conqueror, the Norman descendant of the Vikings who conquered England in 1066.

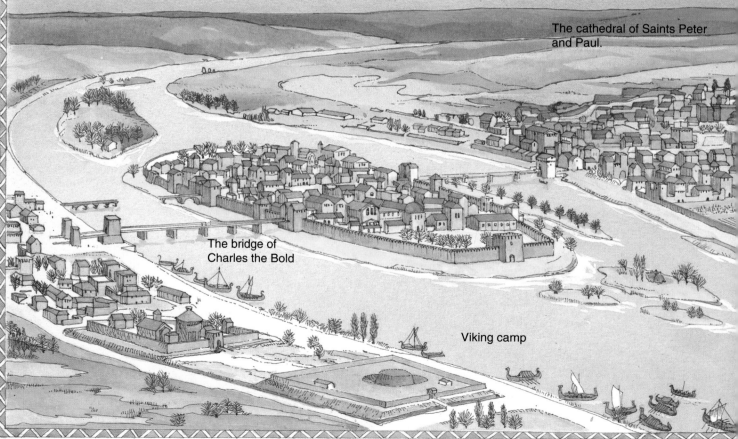

Paris in 885.

The cathedral of Saints Peter and Paul.

The bridge of Charles the Bold

Viking camp

UNDER ROLLO'S SUCCESSORS the Duchy of **Normandy** became larger and more powerful. In 1066 William of Normandy led a strong army and invaded England. He defeated the forces of the English king, Harold, at the Battle of Hastings, from which came his nickname: the Conqueror.

THE AREA where Rollo and his 5,000 Danish Vikings settled was extremely rich. The newcomers, the men from the north or 'Norsemen', became known as Normans and the area where they settled is still called Normandy. The two main towns were Rouen and Bayeux and they are still important.

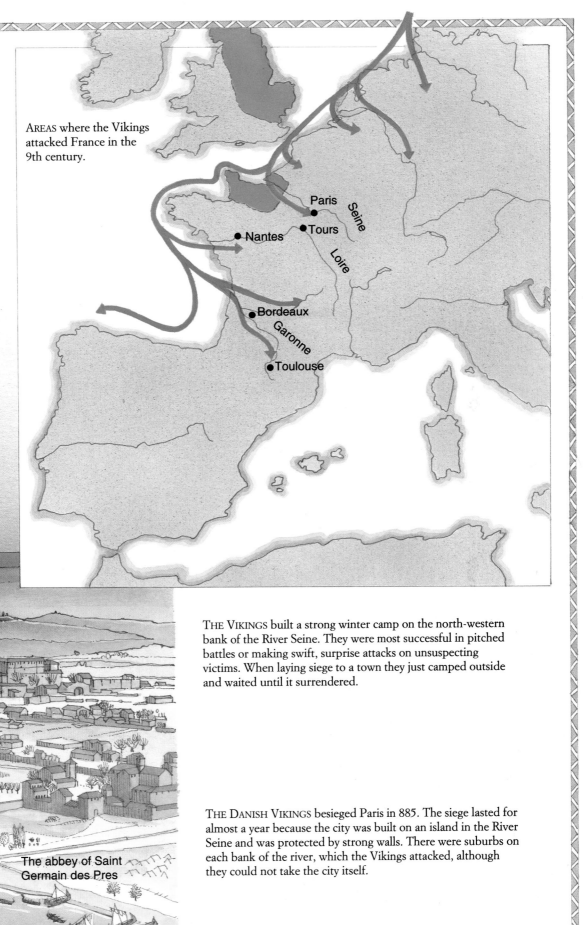

AREAS where the Vikings attacked France in the 9th century.

Paris
Seine
Tours
Nantes
Loire
Bordeaux
Garonne
Toulouse

The abbey of Saint Germain des Pres

THE VIKINGS built a strong winter camp on the north-western bank of the River Seine. They were most successful in pitched battles or making swift, surprise attacks on unsuspecting victims. When laying siege to a town they just camped outside and waited until it surrendered.

THE DANISH VIKINGS besieged Paris in 885. The siege lasted for almost a year because the city was built on an island in the River Seine and was protected by strong walls. There were suburbs on each bank of the river, which the Vikings attacked, although they could not take the city itself.

Mediterranean Raiders

While some Danish Vikings were attacking the British Isles and France, others were sailing further south. Keeping close to the coasts of France and Spain, Danish longships reached Gibraltar and sailed into the Mediterranean. In 844 they attacked and raided the cities of Cadiz and Seville and plundered the north coast of Africa.

Then, around 890, a fleet of about 60 longships entered the Mediterranean. They devastated towns along the south coast of France before heading for Luna in northern Italy.

Loaded with all the things they had plundered, the raiding fleet turned for home. Then disaster struck. A fleet of North African **Saracens** attacked the Vikings near the Strait of Gibraltar. Taken completely by surprise, the Vikings suffered one of their few defeats.

ARAB BOWL decorated with a picture of a Saracen warrior.

IVORY DRINKING HORN made by Arab craftsmen in Sicily, but discovered in York.

THE VIKINGS were decisively defeated by the Saracens in a fierce battle near the Strait of Gibraltar. The Vikings' longships were loaded with plunder and so were not as fast and easy to maneuver as usual. Forty of the Vikings' fleet of sixty boats were sunk, together with most of their crews. No-one can be sure how many warriors died, but even if there were only twenty men in each boat, that means perhaps 800 men were lost. Together with the loss of the boats, this was a major disaster: new boats could be built, but it would take years to replace so many experienced sailors and warriors.

THE SARACENS' ships with their triangular sails were much lighter than the Vikings' drakkars. They were not strong enough for ocean sailing, but in the relatively calm waters of the Mediterranean they were more than a match for the Vikings' boats. The Saracens always tried to fight from a distance, using fire-bombs to set their enemies' boats alight and panic the crews. This tactic was very effective against the Vikings who preferred to get close to enemy boats and leap aboard for hand-to-hand fighting.

The Vikings in Iceland

The Vikings were not just raiders, they were also explorers. The Norwegians, in particular, were short of good farming land. On their overseas voyages they were constantly seeking lands where they could settle and start a colony. The Norwegians made many voyages to explore the north-west Atlantic.

In 815 Floki, a Norwegian, set out from his base in the Faroe Islands to the far north of Scotland. From there he sailed north-west. According to legend, Floki's voyage was long and difficult. Eventually he released two crows. He knew that they would fly towards land, so that all he had to do was follow them. This is what he did and the land to which the birds flew was Iceland.

Many Vikings followed Floki's route. Between 870 and 930 more than 10,000 Vikings are believed to have left their homes in Norway to find a better life in Iceland.

At first the new settlers formed small communities under a single ruler. However, as the population grew, the Vikings divided Iceland into four territories. These were governed by the **Althing**, a general assembly which met each year at midsummer. The Althing made laws that everyone on the island had to obey. Iceland remained independent until 1262, when Hakon, King of Norway, took control of the island.

A Viking farmhouse in Icel

Fish-drying frame

FISH was the most important part of the diet of the Icelandic Vikings. They ate dried fish in the winter when it was too cold to go fishing and also exported it.

MONKS FROM IRELAND had settled in Iceland before the Vikings arrived there.

WOODEN PANELS from a very early Christian church in Iceland.

AS WELL AS FISHING, the Icelandic Vikings reared goats and sheep. Besides meat, these animals gave the Icelanders wool and skins for clothes and milk for butter and cheese.

WOOD was the most important raw material. There were forests of ash and willow in the south of the island. The north was too cold for trees to grow.

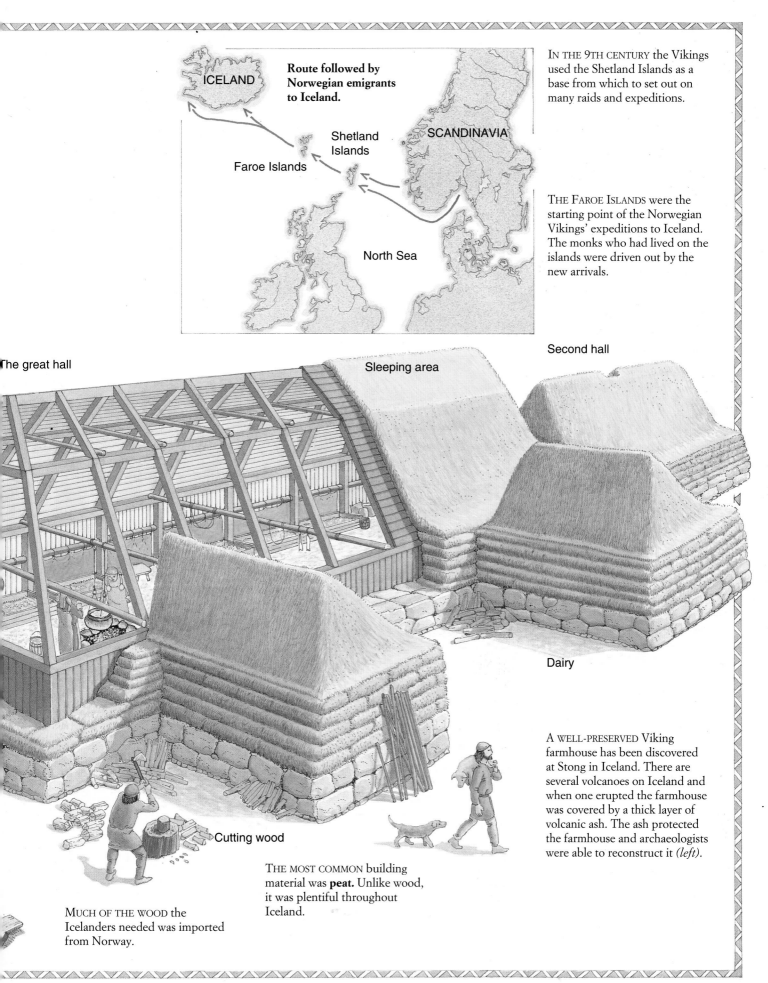

Route followed by Norwegian emigrants to Iceland.

ICELAND

SCANDINAVIA

Shetland Islands

Faroe Islands

North Sea

IN THE 9TH CENTURY the Vikings used the Shetland Islands as a base from which to set out on many raids and expeditions.

THE FAROE ISLANDS were the starting point of the Norwegian Vikings' expeditions to Iceland. The monks who had lived on the islands were driven out by the new arrivals.

The great hall

Sleeping area

Second hall

Dairy

A WELL-PRESERVED Viking farmhouse has been discovered at Stong in Iceland. There are several volcanoes on Iceland and when one erupted the farmhouse was covered by a thick layer of volcanic ash. The ash protected the farmhouse and archaeologists were able to reconstruct it *(left)*.

Cutting wood

THE MOST COMMON building material was **peat.** Unlike wood, it was plentiful throughout Iceland.

MUCH OF THE WOOD the Icelanders needed was imported from Norway.

A New Life in Greenland

FEW VIKINGS could read or write. The only "written" Viking documents that survive are stones carved with **runes,** or letter-like symbols. This one records the Vikings' arrival in Greenland.

LABRADOR

VINLAND

Eriksfjord (Western Settlement)

By 930 the population of Iceland was about 60,000. There was not enough good farming land on the island to grow food for so many people, and the search for new lands became urgent.

In 982 Erik Thorvaldsson, nicknamed Erik the Red from the color of his hair, was sentenced to three years exile from Iceland. He decided to sail west in search of a land that had been glimpsed by an earlier explorer.

After a difficult voyage Erik and his crew came to a rugged, rocky coast. They sailed along it until they reached some sheltered **fjords**. This was the land for which Erik had been searching. He and his men returned to Iceland in triumph.

The next spring, Erik led an expedition of 25 ships to "Greenland" as he called the new land. The ships were loaded with everything needed to start a new life. But there were many storms and only 15 ships reached the west coast of Greenland. There, the Vikings founded their first settlement.

In 1261 the small community on Greenland became a Norwegian colony. But gradually, perhaps because the climate became even more harsh, the population dwindled and the colony finally died out.

GREENLAND is the world's largest island. It is 850,000 square miles in area, but well over half that area is permanently covered in snow and ice, making the island cold and very inhospitable.

Hunters returning home.

THE VIKINGS' WESTERN SETTLEMENT was called Eriksfjord, after Erik the Red. The sea stays frozen from October to May, so life was difficult.

28

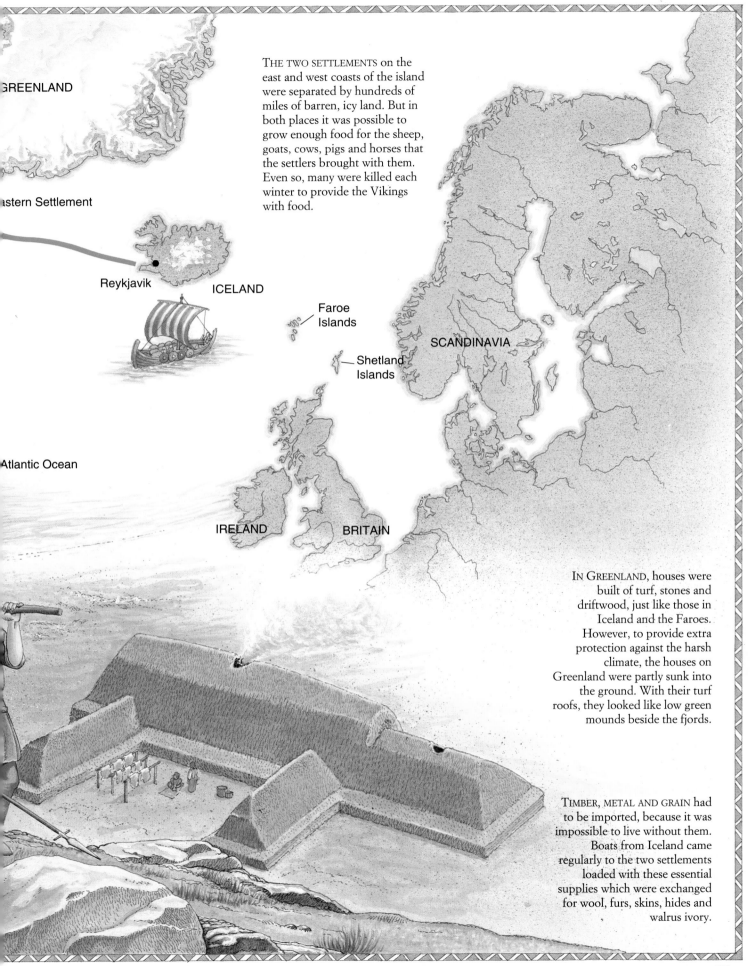

GREENLAND

Eastern Settlement

Reykjavik

ICELAND

THE TWO SETTLEMENTS on the east and west coasts of the island were separated by hundreds of miles of barren, icy land. But in both places it was possible to grow enough food for the sheep, goats, cows, pigs and horses that the settlers brought with them. Even so, many were killed each winter to provide the Vikings with food.

Faroe Islands

Shetland Islands

SCANDINAVIA

Atlantic Ocean

IRELAND   BRITAIN

IN GREENLAND, houses were built of turf, stones and driftwood, just like those in Iceland and the Faroes. However, to provide extra protection against the harsh climate, the houses on Greenland were partly sunk into the ground. With their turf roofs, they looked like low green mounds beside the fjords.

TIMBER, METAL AND GRAIN had to be imported, because it was impossible to live without them. Boats from Iceland came regularly to the two settlements loaded with these essential supplies which were exchanged for wool, furs, skins, hides and walrus ivory.

Life in the Far North

Most of Greenland is extremely harsh and inhospitable. But the Vikings did discover an area of reasonably good land on the east of the island and started a second colony there. Archaeological evidence suggests that the Viking population in Greenland was never more than 3,000.

The settlers lived on small farms around the two main settlements, wherever there were sheltered pockets of better land. But the long cold dark winters and short cool summers made farming difficult. Growing enough hay to feed their animals through the winter was always a problem.

However, plenty of wild animals lived on the **tundra** in Greenland, and that helped the settlers. Besides meat, reindeer, **musk ox** and arctic hares provided skins, antlers and bones for clothes, shoes, needles, tools and weapons. Along the coasts lived seals and **walrus**. They, too, were a source of meat and skins, as well as oil for lamps and cooking. And, of course, there were plenty of fish.

LABRADOR (Markland)

NEWFOUNDLAND (Vinland)

ONE OF THE GREATEST PROBLEMS facing the Vikings who settled in Greenland was the shortage of fuel. There was no wood because it was far too cold for trees to grow. Moss and heather were the only plants that were suitable for burning and they had to be dried thoroughly first.

THE STEFANSSON MAP was copied in 1670 from an old Viking map and shows the North Atlantic as the Vikings knew it. Helluland is Baffin Island, Markland is Labrador and Winlandia (Vinland) is Newfoundland.

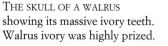

THE SKULL OF A WALRUS showing its massive ivory teeth. Walrus ivory was highly prized.

GREENLAND

Western Settlement

Eastern Settlement

Atlantic Ocean

ICELAND

Hunting walrus in Greenland

AN ICELANDIC BOOK called *Landnamabok* (The Book of Settlement), which was written in the 12th century, gives the location and time it took to reach all the lands where Vikings had settled. This knowledge was lost with the last of the Vikings and many of the lands described in the book remained undiscovered by later European explorers for centuries.

The Vikings in the New World

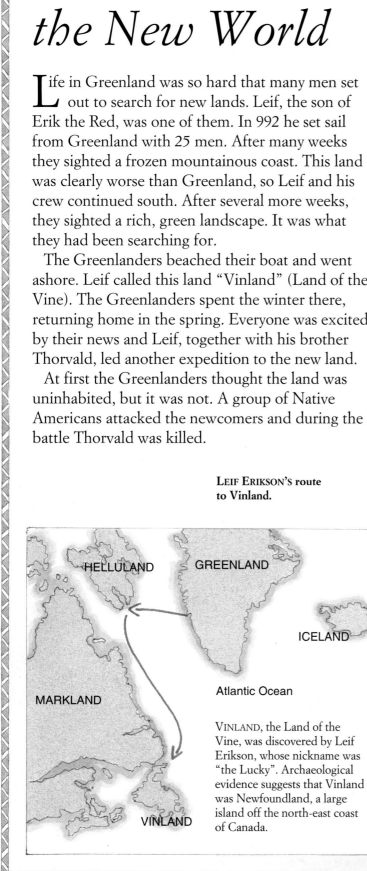

A BALL-HEADED CLUB of the kind the Native Americans used to attack the Vikings.

A TREE BARK HOUSE made by the Algonquin Indians who lived in the area.

Life in Greenland was so hard that many men set out to search for new lands. Leif, the son of Erik the Red, was one of them. In 992 he set sail from Greenland with 25 men. After many weeks they sighted a frozen mountainous coast. This land was clearly worse than Greenland, so Leif and his crew continued south. After several more weeks, they sighted a rich, green landscape. It was what they had been searching for.

The Greenlanders beached their boat and went ashore. Leif called this land "Vinland" (Land of the Vine). The Greenlanders spent the winter there, returning home in the spring. Everyone was excited by their news and Leif, together with his brother Thorvald, led another expedition to the new land.

At first the Greenlanders thought the land was uninhabited, but it was not. A group of Native Americans attacked the newcomers and during the battle Thorvald was killed.

LEIF ERIKSON'S route to Vinland.

HELLULAND

GREENLAND

ICELAND

Atlantic Ocean

MARKLAND

VINLAND, the Land of the Vine, was discovered by Leif Erikson, whose nickname was "the Lucky". Archaeological evidence suggests that Vinland was Newfoundland, a large island off the north-east coast of Canada.

VINLAND

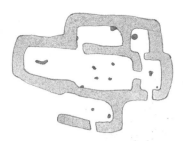

FLOOR-PLAN of Leif's farmhouse in Vinland, which was excavated by archaeologists in Newfoundland.

The death of Thorvald.

LEIF ERIKSON and his men spent the winter in Vinland. Although they were skilled sailors, the winter storms made it too dangerous to risk sailing for home earlier. The new land seemed much more attractive to the Vikings than Greenland.

THE ALGONQUIN INDIANS used weapons of stone and bone because they did not have any metals. However, they outnumbered the Greenlanders and eventually drove them away.

33

The Second Expedition to America

Some years after Thorvald's death another Viking, Thorfinn Karlsefni, set out to repeat the voyage made by Thorvald and his brother. Sometime between 1006 and 1020 Thorfinn sailed westwards with three ships and about 170 men and women, all keen to start a new life in the mysterious, but enticing land.

The voyage was long and difficult. Food supplies ran low and tensions built up between the Vikings in the cramped and by now smelly boats. When the boats eventually reached land it was not Vinland, but a rocky, hostile coast. Disapppointed, the expedition turned south and, at last, they reached Vinland.

The settlers built a camp and started trading with the Native Americans, but relationships quickly turned sour. Soon there was open warfare between the two peoples.

Thorfinn decided Vinland was too dangerous to settle and returned home. The other colonists continued sailing south. Eventually they reached a land called "Hop" and though no-one is sure, this may well have been where New York now stands.

ACCORDING TO THE **SAGA** of Erik the Red, the Native Americans were armed with small catapults. They also used bows and arrows, short spears, **tomahawks** and war clubs.

THE LIGHT CANOES of the Native Americans gave them little protection against the weapons of the Vikings, although both sides suffered losses.

The settlers under attack.

THE VIKINGS showed little respect for the Native Americans, which was one of the reasons that friction soon developed between the two groups. The Vikings had better weapons, but their opponents had the advantage of greater numbers.

IVORY FIGURE of a Native American found in Greenland.

The Vikings in Russia

The Swedish Vikings were traders rather than raiders. When they wanted to find wealth and treasures they did not take to their longships like the Norwegian and Danish Vikings. Instead, they looked to the great landmass that stretched east for thousands of miles. Across this landmass flowed broad rivers, which made traveling very easy. If a river became too dangerous or too shallow for their boats, the Vikings transported them overland.

Around 862 a Swedish Viking called Rurik occupied the village of Novgorod. He fortified it and organized a market. Soon Novgorod was an important political and trade center.

Some years later Rurik's brother, Oleg, occupied the city of Kiev. He transformed it into the capital of a large and powerful state. Oleg was a clever man and his kingdom was rich and stable, and a trade center for goods from all over Europe and Asia.

Like Rurik and Oleg, many Swedish Vikings settled in the lands which they had first visited as traders. One group of settlers was called the Rus – from which the name "Russia" comes.

THE VIKING SETTLERS and the **Slav** people who lived in Russia got on well together. Soon, the two peoples had integrated completely.

Carrying a boat overland.

SILVER PENDANT from a Viking grave in Russia.

IN RUSSIA, Viking merchants traded in all kinds of goods, including precious jewels, spices, silks and glass from North Africa, the **Byzantine Empire** and further east in Asia.

THE FINNS called the Swedish Vikings "Rus", which is how Russia got its name.

BRONZE CLOAK fastener found in a Viking grave in Russia.

NORWAY

FINLAND

SWEDEN

DENMARK

Baltic Sea

RUSSIA

POLAND

MANY OF THE RIVERS had rapids and waterfalls, but the Vikings just carried their boats around these obstacles.

GERMANY

THE DNIEPER AND VOLGA rivers were the Vikings' most important trade routes in Russia.

UKRAINE

THE VIKINGS carried their small boats overland in wooden carriers.

• Kiev

River Don

River Volga

River Dnieper

Caspian Sea

Black Sea

• Constantinople

THE BLACK SEA was the Vikings' gateway to the riches of the Byzantine Empire and countries in the Middle East.

USING ANOTHER NETWORK of rivers and lakes, the Vikings could reach the kingdom of the Bulgars and trading ports on the coast of the Caspian Sea. These were important centers for trade in silver and silks from China, brought by merchants along the Silk Road across central Asia.

THE VIKINGS transported their largest and heaviest boats overland with strong, compact wooden wheels and rollers.

37

Eastern traders

Bases such as Novgorod and Kiev enabled the Vikings to trade ever further east. They built up a network of trading centers and markets throughout Russia. These centers were always beside rivers, because water made transporting goods easy. Although the rivers froze in the long, hard winters, this did not stop the Viking merchants. They just used flat-bottomed boat-sleighs instead of their usual boats.

The Vikings, however, were not the only traders to use these rivers and markets. Merchants from the east, Turks, Khazaks, and even, perhaps, Mongols and Chinese brought their goods to the bustling markets beside Russian rivers, such as the Don, Dnieper and Volga.

Over the years the Vikings built up trade routes as well as trade centers. If they had a good relationship with the local ruler, they were often allowed to settle. The king of the Bulgars, for example, allowed them to build a settlement in return for one in every ten of the slaves they sold on his territory.

SILVER BRACELETS from the Middle East taken by Viking merchants to Denmark.

Viking trading post on the River Volga.

SMALL SCALES used by Viking merchants to weigh gold and silver.

SWORDS made by the Arabs were renowned for their quality and were valuable trade goods.

THE VIKINGS always built
their trading centers on
the banks of rivers
because they provided the
best routes for transport
and communications.
Merchants from many
different countries came
along the rivers to these
centers. They were
attracted by the variety of
goods on sale and the
chance to trade.

THE VIKINGS always made sure
that their trading posts were well
defended. This was another
attraction for the foreign
merchants.

BRONZE CLIP from a sword
scabbard found in a burial
mound beside the River Dnieper.

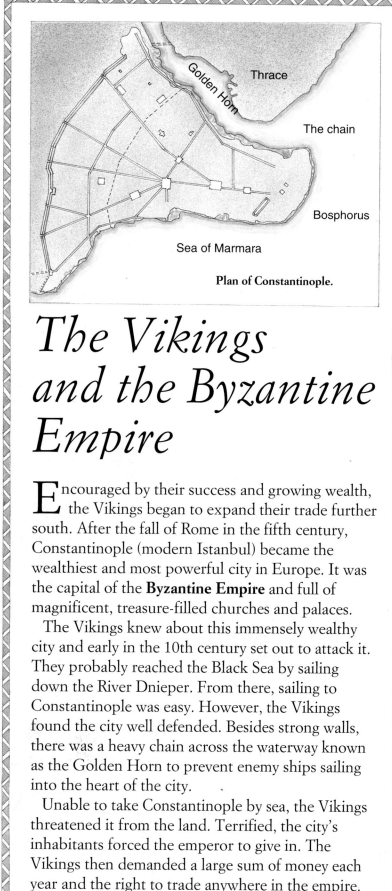

Plan of Constantinople.

The Vikings and the Byzantine Empire

Encouraged by their success and growing wealth, the Vikings began to expand their trade further south. After the fall of Rome in the fifth century, Constantinople (modern Istanbul) became the wealthiest and most powerful city in Europe. It was the capital of the **Byzantine Empire** and full of magnificent, treasure-filled churches and palaces.

The Vikings knew about this immensely wealthy city and early in the 10th century set out to attack it. They probably reached the Black Sea by sailing down the River Dnieper. From there, sailing to Constantinople was easy. However, the Vikings found the city well defended. Besides strong walls, there was a heavy chain across the waterway known as the Golden Horn to prevent enemy ships sailing into the heart of the city.

Unable to take Constantinople by sea, the Vikings threatened it from the land. Terrified, the city's inhabitants forced the emperor to give in. The Vikings then demanded a large sum of money each year and the right to trade anywhere in the empire. In return they would not attack the city.

CONSTANTINOPLE was well protected by strong, high walls with watch-towers at frequent intervals. Sea defense was provided by a chain across the Golden Horn. The only weakness in the city's defenses was its size. It was so large that there were not enough soldiers to defend the walls properly.

ILLUSTRATION from a Byzantine manuscript showing an early type of gun. The Vikings may have had to face such weapons.

ACCORDING to various
accounts of the attack on the
city, the Vikings had an army
of 80,000 men and 2,000 ships.
Even if the ships were small,
this number must be an
exaggeration.

The Vikings attack Constantinople.

THE VIKINGS always held their funerals beside rivers, probably so they did not have to drag the **funeral boats** too far. If the funeral was of a chief it would last for several days, so it was important to hold it close to a well-defended settlement, then no enemy could launch a surprise attack. Once the dead chief's longship was dragged onto the river bank, great piles of firewood were stacked around it. Then the funeral could begin.

A Chief's Last Journey

The Vikings believed in life after death, and the funerals of their chiefs were important ceremonies that lasted for several days.

In 922 Ibn Fadlan, an Arab scholar and traveler, described a Viking funeral he had seen in Russia. Like most important funerals, it took place beside a river. The chief's body was put in a longship, so he could travel to his new life in the way he knew best: by boat. Weapons, clothes and other things he had used in his old life and would need in his new one were put in the boat with him. Then, after several days of funeral rites, a female slave was sacrificed and put on board. Finally, the boat was set on fire. As the boat and bodies went up in flames, the Vikings believed that their chief's spirit was freed to travel to its new life.

The funeral of the Viking chief that Ibn Fadlan described was symbolic of the end of the Viking era in Russia. Just like their fellow Vikings in Britain and France, the Vikings who settled in Russia were quickly absorbed into the local population. By the middle of the 11th century there were few signs of the region's Viking past. The only real clue, then as now, is in the name: Russia.

Funeral of a Viking chief.

ONLY VIKING CHIEFS had elaborate funerals; those for ordinary people were quick and simple. The body of the dead person was put in a small, specially-built boat which was then set on fire.

SETTING the funeral boat alight was regarded as an honor, and the more important the dead person, the greater the honor. Usually the nearest relative carried out the task.

ACCORDING to Ibn Fadlan's description of the Viking chief's funeral in Russia, a special **beer** known as "nabid" was made for the funeral. Large quantities were drunk during the ceremonies and as the funeral boat went up in flames.

TIME CHART

117   The Roman Empire is at its largest.

c230   Neighboring tribes begin attacking the northern borders of the Roman Empire.

313   Christianity becomes the official religion of the Roman Empire.

330   Constantinople becomes the capital of the Roman Empire instead of Rome.

410   Rome is sacked by invading tribes from the north.

c570   Birth of the prophet Mohammed, the founder of Islam.

c650   A funeral ship, full of magnificent treasures, is buried at Sutton Hoo, in Suffolk, England. It will be discovered by archaeologists over 1200 years later.

711   Muslim forces invade and occupy Spain.

742   Birth of Charlemagne.

793   First known Viking raids on the British Isles. They attack the monastery on the island of Lindisfarne.

795   The Vikings attack monasteries on the island of Iona and on the Irish coast.

796   Charlemagne defeats the Avars who had been attacking the eastern boundaries of his empire.

800   The Pope crowns Charlemagne Holy Roman Emperor in Rome.

814   Death of Charlemagne.

815   Floki, a Norwegian Viking, sets sail for Iceland.

843   Charlemagne's empire is divided in two.

844   Danish Vikings attack Toulouse in central France. Another group raids the Spanish cities of Cordoba and Seville and the north coast of Africa.

845   Danish Vikings return to raid French cities, this time attacking Nantes and Tours.

862	Rurik, a Swedish Viking, occupies the village of Novgorod in Russia.
885	The Danes attack and besiege Paris.
890	Large Viking raiding fleet enters the Mediterranean.
911	Charles the Simple of France grants Rollo, the leader of the Danish Vikings, a large area of northern France, which we now know as Normandy.
920	The Muslim traveler and scholar, Ibn Fadlan, witnesses the funeral of an important Viking chief in Russia. He writes a very detailed description of the ceremonies.
930	The population of Iceland reaches about 60,000 people.
982	Erik the Red is sentenced to three years in exile. During this time he discovers Greenland.
986	Erik leads a party of settlers from Iceland to Greenland.
992	Leif Erikson sets sails from Greenland to try to find a land described by an earlier traveller. He discovers the east coast of North America. He calls this new land Vinland.
c1003	Leif and his brother Thorvald lead a party of settlers to Vinland.
1013	Swein Forkbeard of Denmark invades England with his son Cnut.
1016	Cnut becomes king of England.
1027	Cnut invades Scotland.
1035	Death of King Cnut.

1066	William of Normandy, descendant of the Vikings who settled in France, invades England and defeats King Harold at the Battle of Hastings.
c1100	All the lands the Vikings reached are recorded in the *Landnamabok* (Book of Settlement).
1261	Greenland becomes a Norwegian colony.
1262	Hakon, King of Norway, takes control of Iceland.
1453	Constantinople captured by the Turks.
1492	The last of the Muslims are driven out of Spain.
1670	A copy is made of an ancient Viking map showing North America as the Vikings knew it. The original has not survived, the copy, which has, is known as the Stefansson map.

GLOSSARY

Althing
General assembly of the heads of all the families of Iceland. The Althing usually met once a year, at midsummer, to administer justice and make laws.

Auger
Tool like a large corkscrew for boring holes in wood.

Avars
People originally from Mongolia in Central Asia. They had reached southern Russia by the 6th century. They continued to move west, until defeated by Charlemagne in the 9th century. Some of the Avars eventually integrated with the people of what is now Hungary. Others settled in the area that is now Bulgaria.

Beer
The Vikings' most important drink. Nabid, a special type of beer, was drunk only at funerals.

Brazier
A portable metal container holding lighted coals or wood.

Bronze
A mixture of copper and tin. It is very hard and so makes excellent weapons.

Byzantine Empire
The Roman Empire was divided in 395. The eastern part became the Byzantine Empire and was ruled from Constantinople. The western part of the Roman Empire, and its capital Rome, were overrun in the 5th century. This part of the empire collapsed as a result. The Byzantine Empire, however, lasted until 1453, when the Turks captured Constantinople.

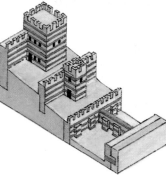

Carpenters
Craftsmen specialized in working with wood.

Caulker
A specialized craftsman who ensures that ships are water-tight. The usual materials for this are pitch, unpicked old ropes and, sometimes, moss and lichen. Because safe boats, seafaring and long voyages were so vital to the Vikings, caulkers were among the most important of their craftsmen.

Cavalry
Soldiers on horseback. Foot soldiers are called infantry.

Chain-mail
Armor made of interlocking metal rings.

Convent
A religious community, usually of nuns.

Crosier
A hooked staff carried by a bishop or archbishop. It is shaped like a traditional shepherd's crook, to symbolize the bishop's care for the spiritual well-being of his people.

Drakkar
A term sometimes used for Viking longships.

Draft
The depth of water required for a ship to float. Viking ships are described as having a very shallow draft because they could float in very little water. This was very useful because it meant they could sail very close to the shore as well as sailing far inland up shallow rivers. It also made them easier to drag overland around obstacles.

Earthworks
A defensive bank of earth built for protection against attack.

Farm
The Viking word for a farm was "boer". Each farm was a small, almost self-sufficient community, with homes, barns, sheds for animals and boats and workshops.

Felt
Thick, dense cloth made by rubbing and pressing wool. Sometimes the hair of other animals is added, and the Vikings may have added hair from the skins of beavers and hares.

Fjord
A long narrow, and often winding, inlet of the sea with steep, high cliffs on each side. Sometimes spelt "fiord".

Foeringer
Small coastal sailing boat used by the Vikings. It could be rowed as well as sailed.

Franks
People of Germanic origin who settled in Gaul in the 4th century. Their most powerful king was Charlemagne. But, in 843, nearly 30 years after his death, his kingdom was divided into two: the kingdom of the Eastern Franks and the kingdom of the Western Franks. Centuries later the eastern part became Germany and the western part became France.

Funeral ship
A ship specially prepared for a funeral ceremony. When an important chieftain died, a large ship was filled with gifts and things, such as weapons and tools, that he would need in his new life. A female slave was killed and put on board, too. Then the ship was set on fire.

Ordinary people had much simpler funerals.

Jerkin
A man's close-fitting jacket, usually sleeveless and often made of leather.

Keel
The piece of timber that runs the length of a wooden boat to which the rest of the boat's framework is attached. The Vikings made the keels of their boats from a single tree trunk, which gave it great strength and flexibility.

Knor
A large boat used by the Viking merchants to carry goods on trading voyages. Much slower than the drakkars, knors were also used by settlers sailing to Iceland.

Lime
A common tree in northern Europe. The wood is light, tough and easy to shape. The Vikings used it for their large, round shields.

Monastery
Group of buildings where a community of monks lives.

Mosque
Muslim place of worship.

Musk ox
Large wild ox that lives in the far north and feeds mainly on moss. It provided the Vikings of Greenland with meat and skins.

Muslims
Followers of the religion of Islam.

Normandy
The area of France west of Paris to the Channel coast. It was conquered by the Vikings, or "the men from the North" at the beginning of the 10th century.

Normans
The Vikings who conquered, settled and then gave their name to that part of France we know as Normandy.

Nose-piece
Part of the helmet that protected the nose. In Viking helmets this piece could be removed.

Pagan
Someone who does not believe in any of the world's major religions.

Palisade
A fence made of strong wooden stakes or posts often placed on the top of earthworks to provide extra defense.

Peat
Densely packed, partly decayed vegetation used by the Vikings to make the walls and roofs of their buildings in areas where there was little wood. They also used it for fuel.

Prow
The front, or bow, of a ship.

Rowlock
Device, usually U-shaped, on the sides of rowing boats to hold the oars in place.

Runes
Letters of a very early alphabet used by the Vikings. Stones carved with runes are the only surviving "documents" from the Viking period.

Saga
A long story passed on by word of mouth, telling the deeds of gods and heroes. The Vikings, who could not read or write, had a very rich tradition of sagas.

Saracens
Muslim nomads who attacked France and Sicily in the 8th & 9th centuries.

Seal
A semi-precious stone carved with a special design which could be pressed into wax to show that a document was official. In the days before people could read and write seals were very important. People, like kings and emperors, had their own seals which they used as we would use our signatures today.

Slavs
Peoples from eastern and central Europe.

Sling
Ancient, hand-held weapon for throwing missiles, usually stones.

Tomahawk
War-axe used by the Native Americans.

Tundra
Vegetation of low bushes, mosses and lichens, found in the north of Europe, Asia and America where it is too cold for trees to grow.

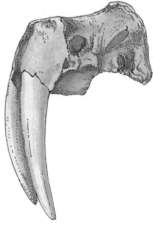

Walrus
Large seal-like mammals that live in the cold Arctic seas. The males' two upper canine teeth grow into long ivory tusks, much sought after by the Vikings.

Yew
Extremely strong, flexible wood used for bows.

INDEX